WALLY LAWSON

HALIF.
MEMOI

Part of the
MEMORIES *series*

Contents

First published in Great Britain by True North Books Limited, England HX3 6SN. 01422 244555
www.truenorthbooks.com | Copyright © True North Books Limited, 2018

Printed and Bound by Short Run Press Ltd, Exeter.
Text, design and origination by True North Books
Part of the 'Memories' compact series and based on the original Nostalgic Halifax publication.

Introduction

One hundred years after Defoe's time, Halifax was in the throes of that massive convulsion we know as the Industrial Revolution. Factories powered first by water, and then by steam, transformed the scale and cost of production. As early as 1837, Anne Lister of Shibden Hall was noting that 'a black canopy hangs over Halifax'. The outsiders' view of Halifax now changed to that 'muck and brass' image symbolised in those famous views from Beacon Hill - a forest of chimneys and a huddle of houses beneath a pall of smoke. The population of Halifax grew from around 9,000 in 1801 to over 100,000 in 1901, by which date it was being referred to as 'the town with a hundred trades'. Industrial dynasties emerged in the nineteenth century, such as the Akroyds and the Crossleys, who amassed unbelievable wealth, but were also driven by a sense of Christian responsibility. The Crossleys, for example, left their mark on Halifax in the huge sprawl of Dean Clough, once the largest carpet manufactory in the world, but also in People's Park and the Crossley Heath School, which began its life as an orphanage.

New Horizons

And now that the black pall has lifted, along with the withering of the old industrial base of Halifax, what do we find? For one thing, a wonderful legacy of stylish and elegant buildings in Halifax and elsewhere which the process of grime removal has now restored to their former glory. We see initiative and enterprise right across Calderdale in the adaptation of old industries (and even mill buildings) and the creation of new ones.

The Halifax Gibbet.

We see a great proportion of the workforce now engaged in retailing and financial services. It is likely that outsiders view Halifax today as somewhere between the vagrants' Hell and Defoe's Paradise. Eureka! - the renowned children's museum and the recently transformed Piece Hall with its rich and varied history, are in the very heart of the town.

Wainhouse Tower Illuminated.

Halifax is a lively, full of character and interest, set amidst the stunning scenery of Calderdale. Many of the photographs in the pocket-sized book are unique to help us recall nostalgic memories of a different era…. Enjoy!

Street scenes

Below: This is a typically nostalgic street scene from the late 1960s. It could be any one of dozens of streets that surrounded the King Cross area. Young children are happily playing out on the cobbled streets, until mom shouts for them to come in. No mobiles, no internet, no computer games or PlayStations back then, children had only the simplest of equipment: jacks, marbles, skipping-ropes, bats and balls to play with, and more importantly, a creative imagination. The car parked on the left, looks like a Morris Oxford or Austin Cambridge, produced around 1960.

Above: Many readers will recognise this picture of King Cross from around 1968. Don't be misled by the vintage pick-up truck in the centre of the image, as it was part of a rally passing through the area. It was one of a number of vehicles and a few people had gathered on the left of shot to see the old vehicles. The buildings and shops were demolished in the 1970s, as part of a new road scheme. Looking at the width of road here, its hard to imagine how they created enough space to build the current by-pass.

HALIFAX MEMORIES

Here we can see in this early photograph from the area of Halifax known locally as Hall End, where Silver Street runs down from the right to link up with both Commercial Street and Crown Street. Pedestrians strolling across the roads at their leisure feature heavily in both images. The sight of horse-drawn carts and the absence of motorcars in these thronging street scenes, suggest the photographs date back to the start of the last century. Prominent in both pictures is Websters, a local firm that ran grocery stores and cafes throughout Halifax. In 1828 George Webster established his tea and grocery business at 3 and 5 Silver Street, and in 1889 he opened the Japanese themed Mikado Café above the shop. Some readers may also remember the Imperial Café, round the corner in George Square, which he also opened in 1908. Webster's went out of business in 1963 and the building was demolished shortly afterwards. A new block of shops and offices was built on the site. The street level shop was subsequently occupied by Jowett & Sowry, stationers, and more recently by a bookmakers.

This 1930s view looking north long Market Street from Union Street is still instantly recognisable, despite the many changes down the decades since the photograph was taken. Along the left of the picture is the bottom side of Halifax's market hall, the finest remaining example of its kind in Britain. In the centre of the scene is the top of Woolshops and the town's oldest remaining shop. Commonly referred to as the 'Tudor' building, suggesting a date in the 16th century, it actually carries a datestone for 1670. Both are probably wrong; the official listing suggests it is 'probably early 17th century'. Almost all of the other buildings along the right hand of the picture were replaced during improvements in the 1970s and 1980s. The schoolboy walking along the pavement on the right is a reminder of the important distinction between boys and men in those days: short trousers versus long. Until the 1960s boys were generally expected to wear short trousers well into their teenage years. Being taken to buy one's first pair of long trousers was an important rite of passage. The first boy into long trousers gained enormous prestige – the last, a sense of shame deep enough to last a lifetime.

This photograph from King Cross, the tramlines are still clearly visible, as are the ornate tram standards carrying the electric power to the vehicles. A single-decker coach can be seen in the distance, heading towards Sowerby Bridge or the Calder Valley road. The photograph was taken in the 1930s and it not be long before motor buses replaced the trams, which had served the town since 1898. The building in the background is the Old King public house, knocked down in the 1970s after 100 years of business, to make way for the new road scheme.

Although the businesses may have changed, this view up Old Market is still very familiar today. It was once used by local traders operating from stalls set up in the busy street. Older readers will fondly remember the shops on the right, such as Burtons and Freeman Hardy & Willis and not McDonald's, Ladbrokes and Subway. The Union Cross, originally called The Crosse Inn because it stood opposite the old market cross, is the oldest inn in Halifax.

Halifax during wartime is caught on camera in this elevated view of Bull Green from 1943. Although in black and white, the distinctive livery of the Halifax Corporation bus and the smoke rising from the cooling towers 'Salt & Pepper' make this scene unmistakably local. The photograph was probably taken from Bull Green House which was opened in 1932. Diagonally across we can see the new Bulls Head public house, which replaced the old building when it was demolished when George street was widened in 1940.

A lorry stacked with bales of hay passes the Star Hotel in Orange Street in the late 1940s. At the time it was a Whittaker's pub and it survived for many years whilst all around it was being demolished and modernised. It eventually closed in 1998 and was later demolished to make way for the Broad Street development. At the bottom of Weymouth Street a man is waiting for his lift with a suitcase and a bundle under his arm. He is across from Allen & Clark and looking in the direction of John Holdsworths, plumber and builders merchants. According to the large bill poster on the wall, the Gaiety Players were performing at the Grand Theatre and 'Vivid Whiteness' was the promise with Oxydol washing powder.

This is a fabulous scene reminiscent of those old Hovis advertisements on television?.... "T'was like taking bread to top of the world. 'T'was a grand ride back though. The advert was actually filmed in Dorset in 1973 but the scale of the task looks very similar in this photograph probably taken some 20 years earlier. Northern scenes such as the one on this photograph, the old Pack Horse Road at Heptonstall, had to be the inspiration behind them. This road, still well used by walkers, was, once upon a time, the scene of a Coiners funeral and the coffin had to be carried up this road by trudging bearers. People living 'on the tops' at one time had chemical lavatories and the 'muck cart' came to empty them. Historically a centre for hand-loom weaving, Heptonstall's cottages and terraced houses are characterised by large first-floor windows to maximise the light for weaving. This picture shows Hebden Bridge in the background and the distinctive sight of houses built on the steep sides of the valley.

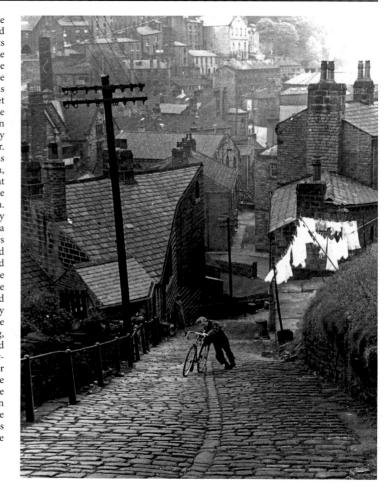

As the name suggests, Commercial Street was one of the main centres for business when it was laid out in the Victorian era. Its creation was authorised in 1853, but work on its development did not begin in earnest for nearly another 30 years. Some established property was razed and the land cleared. Running from Waterhouse Street to Portland Place, it finally opened along its full length towards the end of the century. It was still no more than a decade or two old when this picture was taken. Yet, even by then, Commercial Street seems to have become well established. Many of the town's banks and financial institutions opened at various locations here. The most famous name, 'the Halifax', came to life on this thoroughfare. Halifax Permanent Benefit Building Society, the largest of its type in the land, moved its headquarters to Commercial Street in 1921.

Whiteley's corner, named after the long established newagents and tobacconists featured here which later became involved in the retail travel trade. The shop stood on the corner of Bethel Street and Huddersfield Road, Brighouse. Bethel Street was formerly known as Brighouse Lane (1855). Part of the street, up to Bradford Road, was renamed Police Street (1881). The street was widened in the early 1900s. This picture dates from 1957. Barclays Bank can be seen on the right and the Pentacostal Hall and Albion Restaurant can be seen further along the same side of the road. The Morris half ton van approaching the crossing is the type favoured by the Post Office for many years. Vehicles of this era always seem to have more character than their modern equivalents.

To walk down the familiar cobbled slope of Woolshops is to walk down one of the town's most altered streets. Many readers will remember this view of the top of Woolshops, with K M Lent Ltd, house furnishers on the left and Modelle fashion house on the right and the clear view of the Parish Church in the distance. We can see from the early Bond minicar 3-wheeler and the Ever Ready batteries wagon that traffic could come and go freely up and down the street in the days before it was pedestrianised. The Modelle store was part of the Prince's Arcade and was well known for the quality of ladies designer clothing it offered, so much so that they claimed their stock was replenished from day-to-day deliveries direct from London. Local women will remember that Modelle 's used to be the place to go for that wedding outfit or special dress for works dinner dance. In today's picture we can see WH Smith have taken the majority of the site, after the arcade was demolished in 1983 and that trees and seats have replaced the small island and telephone box.

S treet names or districts usually tell a story, and this 1940s view of Bull Green looking towards Cow Green seems to speak for itself from that point of view. Bull baiting in earlier centuries is a possibility. What is more certain is that the area was once alive with the hustle and bustle of Halifax's cattle market. To complete the agricultural picture, the far end of Cow Green used to be known as Swine Market. The Grand Junction Hotel can be seen just in front of the

tower of the Ebenezer Church. The hotel stood on the site of the old Swine Market until its demolition in 1968. Then again, of course, the dreaded Gibbet once stood at where Gibbet Street used to run into Cow Green. Traffic is fairly light on the photograph, but it is still surprising to remember that this route along the top end of Halifax was the main one for westbound traffic, or for those coming from that direction towards Leeds and Bradford.

This view of the Cross in Elland from Southgate has changed little since the photograph was taken over 60 years ago. Although the businesses have naturally changed, the buildings still remain intact. The Lloyds Bank building was built around 1894. The biggest difference is probably the tree in the centre of the picture which has matured and grown above the height of the church. Parts of the Parish Church of St Mary The Virgin date back to the 12th century. Most of the present church dates from the 13th and 14th centuries and is now Grade 1 listed. St Marys was formerly a daughter of the parish church of Halifax. This part of town got its name from the simple wooden cross that stood on the site where the church was built. Next to Forrest's drapers, the buildings down to Northgate are more easily recognisable to many as Scallywags and the Bodega Bar from the 1980s onwards and more recently The Caddyshack.

With Coronation Street off to the left, Southgate in Elland is pictured as it looked in about 1935. Until 1910, the Post Office occupied the premises opposite the Royal George that are here home to the Liverpool Stores that moved from 22 Westgate. Central Bazaar, where H Littlewood once traded, occupies 39 Southgate. The advert for Brooke Bond tea was a simple statement, without a single chimpanzee in sight. We had our advertising gimmicks and slogans, even during the interwar years, but it was television advertising that advanced the use of jingles and catchy sayings so that some of them became part of our everyday language. Elland is a busy place, just as it was over 80 years ago. As a compact area, space is at a premium and nowadays motorists take great care as they are never sure that a shopper is not about to jump out and off the pavement in front of the car. Nearby Coronation Street is home to something of an anachronism in this day and age. The Rex Cinema continues to operate as a little independent outlet.

HALIFAX MEMORIES

Below: A charming picture of mum and the kids making their way over the Packhorse Bridge. The original settlement was the hilltop village of Heptonstall. Hebden Bridge started as a settlement where the Halifax to Burnley hilltop packhorse route dropped down into the valley. The route crossed the River Hebden at the spot where the old bridge (from where Hebden Bridge gets its name) stands. The bridge was built in 1510. The steep wet hills and access to major wool markets meant that Hebden Bridge was ideal for water powered weaving mills and the town developed during

the 19th and 20th centuries; at one time Hebden was so well-known for its clothing manufacture that it was known as "Trouser Town". Drainage of the marshland which covered much of the Upper Calder Valley prior to the Industrial Revolution enabled construction of the road which runs through the valley. Prior to this, travel was only possible via the ancient packhorse route which ran along the hilltop, dropping into the valleys wherever necessary, as was the case with Hebden Bridge.

Above: Looking up from Old Market, this is 'Shoe Shop Street', as it became known to locals for obvious reasons when you look on the right and immediately spot True Form and Timpsons. Originally this was an 18th century street originally called High Street. With perhaps one exception these buildings are from the Victorian era. This photograph however was taken in 1962 and Crown Street is somewhat changed now, with Dolland and Aitchison on the corner instead of Gledhills gents' tailors, outfitters, hatters and hosiers and Holland and Barrett and Bet Fred replacing the shoe shops. This section of Crown Street is part of the Market Quarter and although the cobbles remain, it is now a pedestrian zone free from traffic apart from certain loading times.

It looks like the chickens have come home to roost in this rare photograph of the steep cobbled road at Winscombe Bank. This track leads from Beacon Hill Road to Old Bank. This road, and Old Bank below were once lined with houses and other buildings. Wiscombe Bank was once part of the Wakefield Gate route, the old packhorse track which passes over and down. It is interesting to see the number of mill chimneys in the distance and the low-lying fog cloud that appears to hang above the town. The young boy looks like he is making his way down the hill in his school uniform to catch a bus to school.

Gazing down Russell Street from Cornmarket towards Market Street in the 1950s saw Halliday's and Halford's on the opposite corner, where WH Smith stands today. On the left hand side of Russell Street, Pinders and Taylor's chemist shop have changed hands, but Neaverson's is still in situ at No5 and in the Old Arcade. With its delightful display of glass, china and other collectables, this business has over a century of tradition behind it in the very same handsome premises. The shop on the far right, where a Burton's branch stands now, belonged to Timothy Whites and Taylors. For many years, this was the main rival to Boots on Britain's high streets, especially in the south of England where it was founded. The Nottingham based company won the day in 1968 when its financial muscle was too great and Boots took it over in a coup that removed its chief competitor from the scene. The cameraman in this photograph had his back to the former Marks & Spencer building, currently used by the Wilkinson store.

Buildings and places of Interest

'Drink Ramsdens and your friends drink with you.' This was the sign above the entrance to one of the town's most respected breweries, a popular landmark which looked out across Wards End for many decades. Ramsden's Stone Trough Brewery is thought to date from the 1730s and was one of the oldest of the many breweries in the district. Ramsden's were absorbed into the giant Joshua Tetley group in 1964 and the site itself was cleared in 1970 to make way for the new H.Q of the Halifax Building Society which opened in 1973. The building on the right of the roundabout at Wards End, was originally known as The Picture House and dates from 1913. It is probably better known to us from 1988, when the building found a new use, as home to the Coliseum nightclub.

This photograph at the bottom of George Street, around the early 1900s, shows a group of elegantly dressed people waiting to board the tram to Highroad Well. Tram services in Halifax started on 29 June, 1898 and ran along three routes from the town centre. Several different and larger sites were in use before the handsome building in this photograph appeared on Commercial Street. The first purpose-built accommodation for the post office was designed by Sir Henry Tanner and opened on 23 June, 1887. It is constructed with the local sandstone at a cost of around £13,000. It was extended in 1926/1927 when the new automatic telephone exchange was installed. Over a hundred years earlier, an office had been established on Winding Road, on the site of what is now The Old Post Office public house and hotel.

As Victorian Halifax grew and civic pride grew with it, it was felt that the town needed a symbol of that pride, a crowning glory almost. The Victoria Hall, seen in this photograph, was built to fulfill that civic desire. A prime location was chosen, the junction of Commercial Street and Fountain Street and the Victoria Hall with its distinctive twin towers was built in 1900 and opened in February, 1901. The floor was designed and built on special springs, which was the modern equivalent of 'state of the art' in those days. The gala opening audience were entertained in their brand new hall by Dr Hans Richter, conductor, and a combined orchestra. The acoustics of the Hall were described as the best in England for choral singing and the Halifax Choral Society gave a performance to put that claim to the test. In 1935 they performed again at the Victoria Hall. This time the world famous local tenor, Mr Walter Widdop, joined them in a performance of 'The Messiah' which was broadcast by the BBC. The Victoria Hall eventually became the Civic Theatre and is now known as The Victoria Theatre.

A rare picture of the Grand Theatre which stood on the Halifax end of North Bridge. The Grand began life as a hotel, became a theatre and, in this picture, has become a cinema. Showing tonight was Douglas Fairbanks Jr in 'Parachute Jumper'. Many a good night out has been had at the 'Grand' and a production of 'Face at the Window' once terrified Halifax audiences. The Globe Hotel, to the right of the Grand, will not be recognised by many readers. It was originally a beer house. Opened in 1897. The pub was used by artistes appearing at the Grand Theatre. Trade was affected by the theatre's closing in 1956. North Bridge which leads off towards Boothtown, from the left of this picture, was opened in 1872. The present two span iron bridge replacing the former old stone bridge which dated back to the 18th century.

The great wide spaces of Savile Park, an area often simply described as the Moor, have been a benefit to generations of local people. At the bottom end of Savile Park a man takes his ease by the drinking fountain in a picture from the 1930s. 'Thank God For Water' and 'Water Is Best' are the inscriptions on the old fountain, a gift to the people of Halifax from Joseph Thorp in 1869, with more than a hint of temperance sentiment about it. On a larger scale the Moor itself was a gift to local citizens, but one which had to be fought for. Skircoat township in the 19th century included Copley and Pye Nest, and was independent of Halifax. Within it fell Skircoat Moor, a precious stretch of common land, and when Halifax proposed to absorb Skircoat, in 1864, what agitated the Skircoat residents most of all was what the Corporation might do to this land. Henry Savile, the Lord of the Manor, supported the 'Skircoat freeholders' and in 1866 he offered the Moor, land worth thousands of pounds, to Halifax Corporation for £100. The condition was that the Moor should remain a 'free, unenclosed ground for the public recreation and use for all time'.

In the picture on the facing page, we can see the fabulous Crossley and Porter building in the background. It was founded as an orphanage in 1857 (see picture left) through capital from Frank (later Sir Francis Crossley, 1st Baronet) and John Crossley, of Dean Clough Mills. In 1887, after a gift of £50,000 from Thomas Porter, a Manchester yarn merchant, the orphanage was extended to include schooling. Over time, the need for an orphanage decreased and the school became a grammar school.

HORSE RIDING
IS PERMITTED ONLY ALONG A STRIP
100 FEET WIDE BETWEEN THE DRINKING
TROUGH & CROSSLEY & PORTER SCHOOLS
ADJOINING & BOUNDED ON THE SOUTH BY
SKIRCOAT MOOR ROAD. AFTER 10AM
ON SATURDAY, SUNDAYS & ALL PUBLIC
HOLIDAYS & AFTER 1·0 P.M. ON ALL OTHER
DAYS.
HALIFAX CORPORATION   (BYE-LAW)

As we can see from the placard there was obviously a need to introduce timing restrictions on the Moor regarding 'horse riding', which only permitted usage along a strip of 100ft wide at certain times of day.

Right: Building work began on the Borough Market in late 1891 and the foundation stone laid in October 1892, but the market was still a year from completion when this photograph was taken in 1895. It was designed in the French Renaissance style by John & Joseph Leeming and erected on the site of the earlier New Market. On 25 July, 1896, the Duke and Duchess of York, the future King George V and Queen Mary, presided at the official opening ceremony - during the same visit that they opened Royal Halifax Infirmary. The hall measures 200ft by 170ft. The central octagon is at a height of 60 ft and is supported by 8 cast-iron columns. A large clock stands above the market stall at the centre of the building. Because of its grand architecture and importance as a feature in the town's heritage, the market is a Grade II listed building. In 2008 it won an award for being the best market hall in the country.

Above: The present railway station in Halifax dates from 1885 and we imagine the photograph was taken towards the end of the 19th century. Halifax station was redesigned during 1884–85, and completely rebuilt during 1885–86. Part of the new station opened on 25 October, 1885, and the remainder on 30 May, 1886. The new station had separate accommodation for LYR and GNR trains, the latter being on the west side. To distinguish it from Halifax St. Paul's and Halifax North Bridge stations, the main station was known from June 1890 as Halifax Old Station. On 30 September, 1951 the name was changed again to Halifax Town, and on 12 June, 1961 it reverted to Halifax.

This is a fabulous view of Shibden Hall and grounds in all its glory. Set in the picturesque Shibden valley, a mile from the centre of Halifax, Shibden Hall dates back to 1420. The Hall is surrounded by beautiful gardens and the estate that forms Shibden Park. At the time of writing, Shibden Hall was the focus of a new BBC drama series written by Sally Wainwright, 'Gentleman Jack' exploring the life of Anne Lister (1791 - 1840) and those who lived in the Hall and Estate.

Ward's Hall was demolished in the first year or two of the Edwardian era. It stood on a plot of land that would then be occupied by a bus station and, later, the Regal Cinema/ABC. Actually, bus station is too grand a description as the spot was little more than spare land in front of a private garage where Hebble buses offloaded passengers. Sir James Stansfield, our longest serving MP, was born at Ward's Hall. In early Victorian times it had been used by Ann Webster, the proprietor of a boarding school for young ladies.

If you will pardon the pun, Francis Crossley (1817-72) made a pile from carpets. He belonged to the family that built the factory complex of Dean Clough Mills. What became one of the world's largest carpet manufacturing businesses was founded by his father and uncle. Francis and his brothers inherited the concern and continued its expansion. He had Crossley House on Hopwood Lane, built in the 1840s. It is, undoubtedly, one of the borough's finest properties. Designed in a style reminiscent of a French mansion, it is a gorgeous reminder of how delightful the world of Victorian architecture could be. After Crossley's death, the property passed into the hands of the Corporation for a nominal figure. By 1890, it had become the Central Library, before incorporating Belle Vue Museum in 1897. The library section was moved to Northgate in the 1980s and Belle Vue Mansion, as many now knew it, became office headquarters.

The horses and carriages drawn up outside the Town Hall in Crossley Street, would date this picture around the turn of the last century. It was designed by Sir Charles Barry and opened in 1863 by the Prince of Wales, the first visit to Halifax by a member of the Royal Family. This Grade ll* listed building has a magnificent 180ft tower and spire which is enriched with sculpture. The building second from right in this picture was the Exchange Restaurant.

Dean Clough is a group of large factory buildings built in the 1840s–60s for Crossley's Carpets, becoming one of the world's largest carpet factories (half a mile long with 1,250,000 square feet (116,000m^2) of floorspace). After years of declining production it closed in 1983, when it was bought by a consortium led by Sir Ernest Hall which developed the Grade II listed site for various commercial and cultural uses. It is now seen as a leading example of successful urban regeneration. Dean Clough is a 20 acre site that stretches half-a-mile in length. There are 19 discrete buildings in the complex, eight of them being 19th Century mills that would impose upon most town centres. The converted mills now house about 150 large and small businesses, along with art galleries, restaurants and the Viaduct Theatre where the Northern Broadsides theatre company is based.

Events & Occasions

These Halifax supporters at Wembley in 1939 look in good heart and rightly so, for the Thrum Hallers were about to record a handsome victory over Salford in the Challenge Cup Final. Nobody outside Halifax expected it, and so success was so much the sweeter. Although no less enthusiastic, supporters were more restrained in those days - no painted faces, replica kit or huge banners. You might sport a rosette, but otherwise a trip to Wembley was a 'dressed-up' occasion. After this 1939 success, these supporters would not have believed that the next Challenge Cup victory at Wembley would not be until 1987 - a nail-biting triumph over St Helens. In between would come defeats at the final hurdle against Bradford Northern in 1949, Warrington in 1954 (after that famous replay at Odsal), and St Helens in 1956. Nevertheless, older supporters will never forget the great team of the 1950s with that powerful front row of Wilkinson, Ackerley and Thorley, half-backs Dean and Kielty, and flying wingers Bevan (or Freeman) and Daniels. The last three were Welshmen and Halifax used to prosper from the 'Welsh connection', particularly with regard to Griffiths, Owen, and James, all top-class full-backs, not forgetting that star forward, Colin Dixon. More recently, brilliance has been provided by players such as Australian, Graham Eadie and New Zealander, John Schuster. And as for Joe, many fans are grateful that 'Kilroy was here'.

A nasty little bug was released by the government in the early days of World War II. It was a propaganda cartoon figure covered in swastikas and was called the 'Squander Bug.' The insect popped up everywhere to remind people that money spent, or squandered, on luxuries could be put to better use by purchasing War or Defence Bonds. The cost of fighting the war was huge, and year by year massive fundraising campaigns were staged in towns and cities across Britain to persuade people to invest in bonds and certificates. Parades were always a feature, and this photograph of 1940 shows Red Cross nurses and the St John Ambulance Brigade winding their way along Cow Green and turning smartly left at the old Crown and Anchor at Bull Green. This may well have been associated with War Weapons Week and the aim for Halifax was to raise at least £1 million, enough for three destroyers. The big inducement also was that the money was being lent to the government, not given, and even a £5 bond would pay for a five inch shell. Halifax War Weapons Week raised £2,562,939, or the staggering sum of over £26 per head - a record for the country, until Elland beat it the following year.

This popular little boy surrounded by caring nurses and cuddly toys is on Rawson Ward at the Royal Halifax Infirmary, during or just after the Second World War. This ward was described as 'Open Air' because all the windows could be opened onto the veranda and some of the children, dependant on their ailment, slept on the veranda. What appears to be a drip stand beside the little boy's bed could have been there to give him fluids. There were no antibiotics in those days and Penicillin was only just becoming widely available. The Royal Halifax Infirmary was built on voluntary donations and the plaques on the wall outside each ward carried the name of the benefactor. The RHI was opened on 28 April, 1896, by the Duke and Duchess of York, who also opened the town's Borough Market that day. It is the Royal Halifax rather than the Halifax Royal because the Duke made a mistake when declaring the building open! Just over a hundred years later the building would be closed and some parts turned into residential use.

There is no mistaking the enthusiasm of the crowd as an unmistakable figure catches a bouquet of roses during his visit to Halifax in June 1945. An enormous audience of 20,000 people had packed itself into the area below Lister Lane, filling Silver Street, Cow Green and Bull Green to greet Winston Churchill. Having provided the inspired leadership that had successfully united the British nation against Hitler, Churchill was now on the election trail in Halifax to support the local sitting Conservative MP, Mr Gilbert Gledhill. It was noted by the 'Courier and Guardian' that Mr Churchill's welcome was 'warm but not effusive', and although the crowd listened attentively to his 20 minute speech, there were a few signs of disagreement when he called for three cheers for Mr Gledhill. Immediately after the speech, Winston lit a cigar, gave his famous 'Victory' sign, and proceeded on his way. Churchill also visited the Calder Valley towns, lunching at Scaitcliffe Hall, Todmorden. It is hard ti imagine that within weeks of the end of the war in Europe, Winston Churchill, saviour of the free world, had been kicked out of office by an apparently ungrateful nation in a Labour landslide. Defeated Gilbert Gledhill declared it was "a tragedy that after all Mr Churchill's efforts in the war, affairs should go against him". It was far from the end for the Tories or for Churchill, of course. At the General Election of 1951 the Tories were back in power with 321 seats to Labour's 295 and Churchill was Prime Minister for the second time.

Although the war was over, these proud soldiers still wanted to make an impression. Spit and polish was no doubt the order of the day for these men of the Duke of Wellingtons Regiment on this very special occasion. Rifles will have been cleaned, buttons and brass made to gleam, berets adjusted to just the right angle and belts 'blanco'd' to perfection. Field-marshal Viscount Montgomery of Alamein, Chief of the Imperial General Staff, is seen in this photograph on a routine visit to 33 PTC, (Primary Training Centre), at Wellesley Barracks on 3 November, 1947. This same visit to Halifax included an inspection of the Royal Army Service Corps, Ovenden Camp. At the time this photograph was taken Field-marshal Montgomery held the rank of general. The soldier shaking hands with the General is well decorated as can be seen from the medal ribbons on his chest. The Halifax Courier and Guardian of the time reported a little known link between the Field-marshal and Halifax. To quote the newspaper, 'His mother was the daughter of Dean Farrar, famous author of 'Life of Christ' and 'Eric', who in turn was the grandson of Jonathan Farrar the Luddenden and Warley clock and watch maker.'

HALIFAX MEMORIES

A very special occasion and Sunday best was the order of the day for these children, posing for a photograph outside the Halifax General Hospital. All the girls have a ribbon in their hair and the boys too have made an effort to look their best. An official air is added to the scene by the presence of the Mayor in the background. On the right of the picture, the scarf-like white headgear of the senior nurse would indicate an Assistant Matron at the Halifax General Hospital. The building in the background, the gravel in the foreground and the presence of nurses adds strength to the opinion that this photograph was taken at what used to be the front entrance to the Halifax General Hospital. In 1930, the site was taken over Halifax County Borough and became St Luke's Hospital, then after 1948 it joined the National Health Service as Halifax General Hospital. The kids all look at peace in this photograph, but who knows whether it lasted after the cameraman had finished taking the pictures.

Leading the way for the Duke of Wellington's 382nd Field Regiment, is Lt-Colonel JF Crossley, MBE, TD, in his comet tank. A rare sight on the streets of Halifax, we can see the tanks passing the top of Crown Street on their way to a display in Manor Heath as part of the Regiments 25oth anniversary celebrations. An estimated crowd of 5,000 watched the display in the park. The feeling of belonging which has always existed between the 'Dukes' and the people of Halifax probably dates back to the 1760s. Lord Cornwallis, commanding troops in the American War of Independence, decided upon the West Riding as the area from which he would recruit men into his regiment, the 33rd Regiment of foot. From that moment on, the regiment became tied to this area and known as the 33rd or 1st Yorkshire West Riding Regiment. The Duke of Wellington's Regiment Museum is based at Bankfield House.

This was the scene on one Sunday evening in July 1906, when tram Number 94 went out of control as it travelled down New Bank and overturned on North Bridge, killing two people and injuring up to a dozen others. Further casualties were avoided when 30-year-old Constable James Dixon, on point duty at the bottom of New Bank, saw the tram rushing down the hill and shouted to pedestrians to get off the tracks. It is believed that July 1st had been rainy and the rails were wet, and it was suggested that this alone was the cause of the derailment. The driver, Theodore Chadwick, was found to have applied the brakes incorrectly and was dismissed after the accident, and, although an inquest cleared him of all blame, Halifax Corporation refused to reinstate him. It is reported that this action triggered off the Halifax Tram Strike. The strike started on 22 August, 1906, and lasted just over three weeks. To counter the strike 20 drivers were brought in from out of the area and as a direct response a 13,000 signature petition was presented to the Town Council objecting to the Tramways Committee's action. With little or no impact, 40 drivers returned to work by 15 September and the strike ended.

The Halifax Zoo & Amusement Park in Exley, opened at Whitsuntide, 29 May, 1909, a venture of Alfred McKill of Leeds. It stood on the site of Chevinedge mansion at what is now Chevinedge Crescent, Exley The opening ceremony included the King Cross Band conducted by Arthur O. Pearce. A 17-year-old Indian elephant which took part in the opening ceremony was alarmed by a tram and bolted as it came down Salterhebble Hill, and frightened the crowds before stumbling and falling over. Almost 50,000 people visited on the opening weekend. This was a popular attraction at weekends and holidays with the zoo – there was a pygmy farm with miniature buildings and small animals – a monkey house, an ostrich farm, aviaries, a bandstand, and a lake with a fountain. The zoo aimed to represent the world's range of animals, and exhibited more than 1,000.

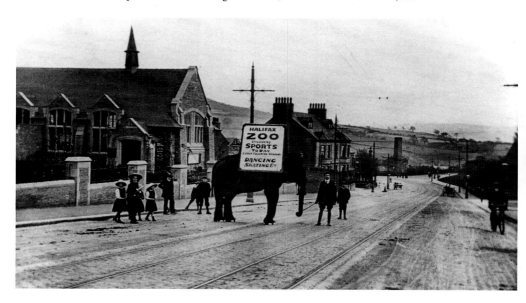

It is January 1983 and the 'Iron Lady' is in town. She can be seen here talking with Production Manager, Malcolm Robertshaw, in the Pre-Press department at the Evening Courier. A very young looking Roger Bates is concentrating intently, as he inputs the latest news from the days events. High security surrounded Margaret Thatchers' two hour visit to the local newspaper offices on Regent Street. After the Falklands War, Mrs Thatcher had gained a new found popularity, and riding on a wave of patriotic enthusiasm and increased support the government gained a landslide victory at the general election held on 9 June, 1983. Only a few days before this picture was taken she had visited the Islands to see at first hand the programmes of rehabilitation and development, seven months after the war. Maggie can be seen with a rare smile in this photograph, which perhaps indicates she had a glimpse of future headlines.

That elusive and elegant piece of silverware is being held aloft by members of the victorious Halifax Rugby League Team in May 1939, as a specially adapted bus took the team and the cup through the crowded streets to the Town Hall for a civic reception. The Rugby League Challenge Cup had been carried home from Wembley by train. Given little chance by the sporting pundits, Halifax had brushed aside a powerful Salford team to win the final 20-3 in front of a 57,053 Wembley crowd. Salford had not previously conceded a try in the Challenge Cup of that season, but Halifax crossed their line four times, the try scorers being Smith, Bevan, Treen and Todd. Captain of the team, Harry Beverley, led by example and described the triumphant return to Halifax as 'one of my proudest and happiest moments'. An estimated crowd of 100,000 packed the streets of Halifax to welcome home their heroes. The photograph shows the progress of the bus at the Bull Green stage, with the Plummet Line Hotel clearly visible in the background. 'Here come the conquering heroes', was the proud message on the front of the bus.

Royal Visits

When King George VI and his Queen Elizabeth, later the Queen Mother, visited Halifax in October, 1937, the Queen wore a two piece dress in a beige-pink pastel shade with a three-quarter length coat trimmed with fox fur. She wore a modern hat with a high crown which was trimmed with light fawn velvet. The royal couple, seen here outside the Town Hall, were spending a few days visiting Yorkshire and, on the day they came to Halifax, 20 October, a 21-gun salute roared out a welcome from Beacon Hill and smiling, waving crowds thronged the route. The Royal couple stayed with the Princess Royal and Lord Harewood at Harewood House for the duration of their visit to Yorkshire, and the Princess Royal accompanied them to Halifax. The Princess was a regular visitor to our town and massed schoolchildren cheered and waved at the royal party when they drove along Savile Park.

Two years after her marriage, the then Princess Elizabeth visited Halifax for the first time. On 26 July, 1949, the royal limousine made its way through the streets of Elland. On a sunny day, crowds lined the streets to cheer and wave as the 23 year old Princess and the Duke of Edinburgh drove by. Locals turned out en masse to cheer the couple and enjoy a moment when they could forget their woes only a few years after the end of the Second World War.

Whathat better than a royal visit for that little bit of joy? She and Prince Philip captured the hearts of the people during their two-hour visit in July, which was part of a three-day tour of the industrial West Riding. She was given a baby outfit in pale blue wool for her young son, Prince Charles, and a box of sweets. The royal tour of 1949 set Yorkshire alight with enthusiasm for the beautiful young Princess.

The Princess visited the Reflecting Roadstud factory during her 1949 tour of Calderdale. Standing behind her on the far left is the man who helped revolutionise road safety in the 1930s with an invention that, with certain modifications, is still widely used today. Percy Shaw (1890-1976) was born at Lee Mount, before moving as a toddler to Boothtown, where he would spend the rest of his life. He began experimenting with designs and, in 1935, set up his company to manufacture reflective road studs that could be used in different positions on a highway to mark out its centre or edge. A patent was granted the following year. The reflective lenses were forced into a rubber housing when a wheel passed over them and then popped out again in a self cleaning action. The cat's eye nickname stuck and the widespread adoption of Shaw's invention must have saved many thousands of lives on our roads during the wartime blackout and the years since.

Princess Elizabeth looks a little pensive during the 1949 royal visit to Halifax. Perhaps it is the tight schedule she has to keep, as she came to the town with her husband, the Duke of Edinburgh, for just a two-hour visit. The visit was part of a Royal tour of Yorkshire, which included various Yorkshire towns including York, Wakefield and Huddersfield. Thousands of schoolchildren had gathered at Spring Hall in the hope of seeing the future queen at close quarters. The schoolchildren were given time off from their lessons so that they could demonstrate their support for the monarchy. When the 23-year-old Princess came past they waved little flags on sticks and hollered as loudly as they could. To see a celebrity in the flesh was something special. There was no television for these children, so they had only been able to get glimpses of members of the royal family through occasional newspaper photographs or clips on a newsreel at the cinema. To see a special person in close up was a treat indeed.

Halifax Memories

Halifax was honoured by a royal visit in 1937 when King George VI and Queen Elizabeth came to see us and visit Shibden Hall. Despite being the consort, it was the former Elizabeth Bowes-Lyon who took the lead in this photograph, much as she did in life. Although he was the head of state, she was a definite driving force behind the throne. After a sedentary tour of Shibden Hall, King George VI and Queen Elizabeth are met by large cheering crowds, as well as having to greet countless local dignitaries. They also get treated by Australian Rugby League Team to a performance of their now defunct Aboriginal War Cry. King George VI and Queen Elizabeth are on a Yorkshire tour, having visited York the day before, as well as Bradford. George VI was regarded as a reluctant king after his brother Edward abdicated the previous December. He had engaged Lionel Logue to help with his stutter in October 1926, just before the first sound newsreels. After his death of coronary thrombosis in 1952, the queen mother survived her husband by an astonishing 50 years.

The Piece Hall

Described as an "architectural and cultural phenomenon", The Piece Hall dates back to the Georgian era. It was built as a cloth hall for handloom weavers to sell the woollen cloth "pieces" (30-yard lengths of woven woollen fabric produced on hand looms) they had produced and opened on 1 January, 1779, with 315 separate rooms arranged around a central open courtyard. A centre of the cloth trade, Halifax had a Cloth Hall and a Linen Hall for many years and businessmen who came to sell or buy cloth had long been in the habit of lodging at certain inns, but the fine new Piece Hall was built at the expense of local clothiers, on land provided by the Caygill family.

It was seen that bringing merchants and buyers together in one place would create a more competitive and efficient market and discourage fraudsters. Trading took place every Saturday between the hours of 10.30 am and 2.30 pm when a bell would signal the close of the market. Cloth was transported from the surrounding valleys by packhorse or horse and cart and unloaded in the courtyard where provision was made for one 'parking place' per person.

The small rooms around the perimeter were used by buyers and sellers to carry out their business. Those less well-off and unable to cover the cost of renting a room, could site themselves on the grass in the courtyard. The rooms are on three levels on the eastern side which, due to the slope of the ground taper away to two levels towards the west. The bottom gallery is known as the 'Arcade,' the one above is the 'Rustic' and the top one is the 'Colonnade.'

Amazingly, the life for which the Piece Hall had been designed and built lasted only 2 years when the industrial revolution arrived and spinning, weaving and dying mills sprang up all over Yorkshire and the machines they introduced took over the independent weavers' jobs. This resulted in a shift away from small producers and traders, with new larger mills in the Halifax area trading directly with merchants and exporters.

Other West Yorkshire textile manufacturing towns and cities all had their own halls, but the mills were able to produce textiles quickly, efficiently and more consistently than an individual working from home, added to that a network of canals and railways slowly appeared opening up markets far and wide all of which made working from home impractical and inefficient, and cloth halls became monuments to an earlier age.

After years of decline, The Piece Hall was acquired from the trustees in 1868 by Halifax Corporation. They converted it into a wholesale market hall and some of the small rooms were combined to make larger shop units; cellars were created and the south pedestrian gate was enlarged to allow vehicles to enter the courtyard with Iron Gates installed over the entrance (supplied by George Smith of the Sun Foundry, Glasgow for £120). Sheds and latrines were constructed in the courtyard.

The iconic building and its historical importance at the historic centre of the world's woollen trade, was awarded Grade I listed protection on 3 November, 1954, and remains as the last Cloth Hall in Britain.

In 1971, after The Piece Hall had become seen as unsuitable for a wholesale market, the businesses were dispersed elsewhere throughout the town and demolition of the then two-century-old building was considered. Government grants were made available and the Halifax Corporation received funding to make the building a tourist attraction. The sheds that had been built in the 19th century were demolished and the courtyard landscaped; further, walls were removed from the original rooms to create shops, and a new museum – art gallery was opened on the east side. The new Piece Hall opened on 3 July, 1976.

Since 2013, thanks to funding from Calderdale Council and the support of the Heritage Lottery Fund, with additional support from Garfield Weston Foundation and the Wolfson Foundation, a project has been undertaken to renovate the whole of The Piece Hall, creating a new cultural quarter for Halifax.

After shop owners had moved out, the building was closed for redevelopment on 16 January, 2014. A three-storey extension was added to the south-east corner close to the Square Chapel. After the massive project was eventually completed The Piece Hall re-opened on 1 August, 2017. The 66,000 sq ft open-air piazza, combines bars, restaurants, cafés and shops. It also has a heritage centre featuring stories of Georgian Halifax. The Courtyard is intended to host a programme of events including concerts, theatre, markets, sporting events and an ice rink. And fittingly, one room has been kept as it was originally, to help retain the strongest possible link back to the building's history.

Birds Eye View

This photograph, which is well over 65 years old, somehow manages to foreshorten the distance between Barum Top, looking down Rawson Street to the imposing Halifax General Post Office at the bottom. Southowram Bank can be seen in the background winding up a barren Beacon Hill with familiar Halifax view of the little house against the skyline. Unusually, a mounted policeman can be seen in the centre of this photograph and the need for his presence is unclear. The Olympia Garage car sales, service and repairs business is in the centre of the picture. The property was demolished around 1999 and a Wetherspoons pub named The Barum Top Inn is now on the site. These days the placards on the right of the picture have been replaced by a multi-storey car park and the latest trendy bar. The former Comet store at Barum Top became a pub, known successively as the Barcentro, then the Barracuda in February 2002.

ailways and coal dominate this view, along with the more elegant lines of North Bridge, a
veritable icon of Halifax and one which has graced this busy part of the town since 1872. The
graceful two-spanned structure replaced a stone bridge which had served travellers for over
a century. Many of the features shown in this picture have disappeared since it was taken in 1967.
The Power Station and the 170 ft tall cooling towers were demolished between 1974 and 1975, the
cooling towers resisting attempts to blow them up with high explosives and later being dismantled
bit by bit. Motoring features strongly in this picture, with Dews Garage's sprawling modern
premises on the right of North Bridge and Cable Motors' triangular property selling Reliant three
wheelers and motorbikes below it.

HALIFAX MEMORIES

This is an iconic snapshot of the streets between North Parade and Northgate at the beginning of the 1960s. All the buildings back to the light coloured Timeform building have gone now, to be replaced by the Broad Street Plaza complex. We can date this picture reasonably accurately as we can see in the bottom right, that work had just started on the foundations for the Albion Court flats which were completed in 1964. The Star Hotel in Orange Street, is central to the photograph and just to the right the purpose-built 28-lane bowling alley was being built. It was opened by Coronation Street actress Pat Phoenix on 6 February, 1964. The two cooling towers in the background, upper right of this picture, known locally as Salt and Pepper were demolished in the mid-1970s. For those readers who liked a meal in town on a night out the Far East Chinese restaurant can just be seen in the top right on Northgate, where the bus station now stands. It was the first Chinese restaurant in Halifax when it opened in 1959.

A rare elevated view of Waterhouse Street and the land beyond, showing the premises of the Yorkshire Bank and the Broadway Supermarket. The triangle of open land towards the top of the picture was used as a car park before the block of offices known as Crown House, and the shops and nightclub running along Broad Street were built. Crown House now dominates the skyscape at the top of Broad Street, with its modern office accommodation on nine floors. The building of Crown House and the adjacent modern shops and nightclub premises took place in 1968 and was completed at a cost of £250,000. The former Crossfield bus station is visible on the right of this panoramic view, which provided the travellers of Halifax with good service for over thirty years, until the new bus station on Northgate took its place. Government offices have since been built on the site.

Below: Very few of our readers will remember that this area at Cross Fields was once a densely populated site known as 'The City'. Built in the 19th century, it was a maze of back-to-back houses on narrow and dimly lit streets. In the photograph above we can see the open area created when 'The City' slums were demolished in 1926. The site stood empty until 1938, eventually making way for the bus station and the Odeon Cinema, which we can clearly see in the other pictures. Also in evidence in the top picture is the classical Oddfellows Hall building which stood on St James Road. The Hall was opened on June 1840 and later became the Alhambra Cinema. In the 19th century Charles Dickens made a guest appearance at the Hall. The building was demolished in 1959 and in subsequent years became a collection point for children catching school buses to Holmfield.

Right: This elevated view of the Broad Street intersection with Orange Street and Waterhouse Street is still very recognisable today, although the left hand side of the photograph has changed dramatically in recent years. On the left, the Brunswick Bowling Alley did good trade for a while. The 10 pin boom of the early 1960s was assisted by some television exposure on ITV's 'World of Sport', but it was not the most gripping of action to captivate Saturday afternoon audiences. For a while, the alley flourished, but later became a cut price supermarket. Since 2012 this has been the site of the new Broad Street Plaza, with restaurants and a Vue Cinema complex, which was probably 14 years in the making. On the right, Halifax Town Hall was opened on the 4 August, 1863, by HRH The Prince of Wales (King Edward VII). The ornate town hall was designed by Charles Barry, who also designed the Houses of Parliament. This Grade ll* listed building has a magnificent 180ft tower and spire which is enriched with sculpture and looks much cleaner today than it does in this photograph.

The unique photograph was taken from the top of the Town Hall, looking along Princess Street with Southgate in the distance. The picture was taken in April 1973 by amateur photographer Cyril Campbell, who was part of the daredevil team painting the Town Hall clock and weather vane. We can date the photograph accurately to 1973 as the pedestrianisation of the Corn Market and Southgate precinct is just about complete.

To the right is the White Swan Hotel, which was opened in 1858 when Princess Street was developed. The original Swan Inn and Posting House, built around 1585, stood on the corner of Crown Street and Princess Street, where Dollond & Aitchison is today. From this rooftop vantage point we can look down on the French Renaissance style Borough Market building, opened in 1896 by the future King George V and Queen Mary. On the corner of Russell Street we can clearly spot the Boots Chemist logo, which many readers will remember as the home of rivals, Timothy Whites and Taylors.

Taken from the top of the Town hall, this photograph shows the area just north of the town centre known as Cross Fields, after the 19th century back-to-back terrace housing popularly known as 'The City' had been demolished. It looks like a bombsite but this area of land marks the site of one of the town's earliest 20th century clearance schemes. Around 780 people lived in insanitary conditions until the area was cleared in 1926. The site remained empty for a number of years until work began in 1937 on a new Odeon Cinema. The cinema arose from the ashes of 'The City' opening in 1938 with a seating capacity of 2050. Later still, in 1954, the Crossfield Bus Station took up the rest of the plot. Many of the buildings in the photograph were to disappear later, including the Alhambra, which was built in 1840 and stood on St James Road until it was pulled down in 1963. Some readers may remember the building as the Halifax Friendly and Trades Club. Its days as a cinema spanned a period between 1917 and 1959. Charles Dickens and Franz Liszt both performed there.

This elevated view looking along Commercial Street was probably taken from a window in Ramsdens Brewery building at Ward's End. Commercial Street dates back to the end of the 19th century. Depending on your age, the building on the right you will recognise as either a cinema or a nightclub. Opened originally in 1938 as the Regal Cinema, it was built on the site of Ward's End Hall and an earlier bus station, designed by William Riddell Glen (1884-1950). This picture was probably captured in the mid-1950s a few years before it became the ABC Cinema. The last film to be shown at the cinema was Spiderman on 25 June, 2002, before closing for redevelopment into a theme bar and nightclub.

The crowd at Odsal Stadium for the 1939 Challenge Cup semi final between Halifax and Leeds was the highest ever recorded in Britain for a rugby league match. Stated here as 66,308, it is reported in Bradford Northerns (now Bulls) records as the attendance being only 64,453. Perhaps we have to take the figures with a pinch of salt because the match was played on All Fools Day, but what is not in question is the commitment of both sides. The goal was the trip to Wembley and an opportunity for supporters to stroll down the Way into the magnificent stadium a month later. Halifax won the day in front of this large crowd and went on to meet Salford. At that time, Odsal was a relatively new ground, having been bought by Northern as a former quarry and tip site in 1933. The site was transformed and the first game held there on 1 September, 1934. Halifax played at Odsal again in front of an even larger crowd when another new record attendance of 102,569 fans came to see the Challenge Cup Final replay with Warrington in 1954.

Halifax Memories

It's the bleak mid-winter at the Shay, the grimness of the day being enhanced by bristling mill chimneys and the barren wastes of Southowram Bank in the background. This is a rare photograph from the FA Cup Fifth Round tie between Halifax Town and Tottenham Hotspur in 1953. A difficult 5th Round FA Cup tie was anticipated as Halifax, in the old 3rd Division (North), had overcome two 1st Division sides, Cardiff and Stoke, in the earlier rounds. Long-standing Town supporters will well remember the half-back line of Geddes, Packard and Moss, with goal scorers such as Darbyshire and Priestley up front. The match was in doubt due to overnight snow but the pitch was cleared sufficiently for it to proceed although blue dye had to be used for the pitch markings, in front of a massive crowd of 36,885. The illustrious Spurs team, containing such great names as Alf Ramsey and Bill Nicholson, scored three second half goals to give Spurs a convincing victory.

Work, Rest & Play

Pictured standing at the doorway of 15 Bank Street, in Todmorden. With him is his second wife, Sarah, alongside his four daughters from his first marriage – Ellen, on the far left holding the baby, together with Mary, Patience and Sarah. The back-to-back house at Bank Street would be the Stansfield family home for the next two generations. Back-to-back housing was a pragmatic approach to the acute housing shortage of the latter half of the 19th century. The ever increasing population of the North's industrial towns and cities led to more and more folk being crammed into smaller and smaller spaces. Tens of thousands of speculative, often jerrybuilt, back-to-back houses were constructed. On hilly sites the back-to-back element was also part of an up-and-over building scheme, with 'under dwellings a common feature as well as landing-access only. Most were demolished in slum clearances in the 1960s.

A woman's work is never done. Never has that been more the case than when applied to a rural setting. Out in the countryside, there was no easy life for women who relied on the good soil of England to provide them with a living. They tilled the land with hand tools, fetched in the crops and milked the cows without the help of electrical aids and petrol driven machinery. When day was done, it was back home to face a round of cooking, cleaning and nurturing. At the end of the 19th century life expectancy was just 45 years. The traditional three score years and ten was for those who had a life of privilege. The work that these country girls carried out laid down the foundation for more formal organisations that were required in the world wars that were to come in the 20th century. When the menfolk marched off to fight in 1914 and again in 1939, there was a huge void left behind. In 1915 the Board of Agriculture actively encouraged women to become farm labourers, though traditional male farmers had to be persuaded to accept them. By 1917 some quarter of a million girls and women were working the land. The Women's Land Army was even more formally organised in the Second World War when conscription was introduced.

Among the earliest depictions of the game of 'knur and spell' is this one featuring a match which took place near Rive Rocks above Todmorden around 1890. Matches played on the tops often attracted large crowds of spectators. The game was played between two or more contestants, commonly a local expert and a leading player from another town. The winner was the contestant achieving the longest knock over an agreed number of hits, or by the average knock. The game is thought to have its origins in medieval times and was often played on Shrove Tuesday and Good Friday. But it may be older still: its name derives from the Norse for ball game 'nurspel' suggesting that it may have arrived with the Vikings, though 'spell' is also a dialect word for a piece of wood. Interest in the game reached its height in the 19th century. Though it retains its enthusiast even today, interest dwindled as men became able to afford other sports such as golf. Soon after this photo was taken Todmorden Golf Club was formed at Todmorden Edge on the uplands overlooking Centre Vale Park.

Work in the winding room at Joshua Smith's Frostholme Mill, at Cornholme, came to a brief halt for the photographer to capture this image. At one time this large cotton mill employed more than 700 people, making it one of the area's major employers. The firm of Joshua Smith operated the mill for over 70 years, from the early 1880s until the 1950s. The photograph was taken in 1913, just a year before the outbreak of the First World War. Clearly the winding of cotton yard onto bobbins was regarded as 'women's work'. In stark contrast with the women in their aprons standing by their machinery is someone apparently rather more senior in the mill – a man wearing suit, collar and tie. Compared to other forms of employment, however, mill work was relatively well paid, and would shortly become even more so. The outbreak of war in 1914 leading to millions of men joining the forces created a huge labour shortage in industry. Women took over many of the jobs previously done by men. Wages rose and big houses were soon denuded of servants who discovered that mill work not only paid infinitely better than the pittance commonly paid to servants, but also gave them the freedom to do what they liked in their own time, a luxury often not granted in domestic service.

A reasonable crowd had gathered to watch St John's ladies cricket team when the photographer took this snapshot of play. Although its a ladies cricket team, they look to be taking on the men, judging by the number of smartly dressed gentlemen surrounding the elegant lady batsmen. The inter-war years witnessed a remarkable blossoming of women's cricket. This development threatened one of the major assumptions about sport, and cricket in particular namely, that it was very much a male preserve. The 2017 England World Cup winning squad may have something to say about that however. The popularity of women's cricket has ebbed and flowed over the decades. Today, women's cricket is once again in vogue, with international teams, in particular, gaining significant coverage in the mass media.

A number of well dressed Edwardian folk can be seen in the top picture, waiting for the show to start at the Electric Theatre (not to be mistaken with the cinema of the same name at Ward's End). The building housed, 'Hall's Tours of the World', a novelty first introduced into London's Oxford Street in 1906, where patrons sat inside a replica of a railway coach watching panoramic views on a screen which gave an illusion of movement. This was thought to be the first of its kind outside London and caused somewhat of a sensation to people who had not seen the like before. The popularity of Halifax Zoo was relatively shortlived, however, as First World War food shortages meant that the animals could not be fed properly and the enterprise closed in 1917.

The annual works outing was a treat that every member of staff would look forward to. Here we see employees from G H Gledhill & Sons Ltd. of Trinity Works at a seaside resort on the east coast. The story of their company starts in 1886 with the invention of an 'automatic cash till' with a mechanism for recording transactions on a roll of paper. The firm's first premises were at Broad Street, but later additions took place with property at Trinity Works (with an extension along Harrison Road) Jubilee, and Victory Works.

A somewhat informal example of maypole dancing taking place in Adelaide Street, Todmorden, in May, 1960. Maypole dancing took place in most neighbourhoods each year on 1 May, with a May Queen being chosen from among local girls. And what excitement and jealously that could raise, with mothers convinced beyond reason that their disappointed daughters were the ones that really had the strongest claim to the throne. The overt symbolism, obvious in previous centuries, was long lost by the 20th century to be replaced by a gentle and civilised folk custom which delighted everyone involved in the annual celebrations. Sadly, this tradition seems to have largely died out as a fixed event in the public calendar, although the practice still continues intermittently. Elsewhere in Calderdale the fact that maypole dancing was once quite literally a central part of village life is commemorated in the name of the Maypole Inn at Warley in the heart of the village.

This is a joyous photograph from any era, of children having fun without a care in the world. Perhaps, Enid Blyton could have used this scene as an inspiration for a new series of books. If she had, then instead of the Famous Five or Secret Seven, there might have been the Tremendous Ten. The nine children, along with Mick the dog, were having a whale of a time on the see-saw, precariously perched on several blocks of stone. No doubt their mums had warned them that it would all end in tears, but youngsters need to take a few risks and experience the odd scraped knee in order to mature. They need to be protected, but not cosseted. The friends had a lovely time playing at the north end of Church Street, Heptonstall, in 1921. So what, if they came down to earth with a bump as they could dust themselves off and start all over again. The buildings in the background, near the White Lion at Town Gate, look exactly the same today as they did in this photograph; as though time stood still!

A lovely view of the beautiful Peoples Park in bloom. People are taking the opportunity to sit and relax on a fine day. The people seated on the benches in this shot are on the terrace, slightly higher than and overlooking the parkland, the fountain and the bandstand. A beautiful park indeed and given to the people of Halifax by Sir Francis Crossley in August 1857 when 10 bands and thousands of people thronged the park to celebrate the opening. Designed by Sir Joseph Paxton who also designed the Crystal Palace, the park was accepted on behalf of the people by the Mayor of Halifax, John Whitworth. A few years later a statue of Sir Francis Crossley was erected in the park. The marble statues on the Terrace of People's Park were designed by G. H. Stokes and sculpted by Francesco Bienaimé. In the background can be seen the magnificent building which was once Belle Vue Library.

Does my bum look big in this? This pretty lass has all the potential for giving lads a tough time. She was obviously well aware of modern fashion. Her knitted two piece was designed more to catch the eye than for practical purposes. The fabric would have got rather heavy and sag somewhat when immersed in the sea. The great British seaside holiday was at it's height during the 1950s and early 1960s. It was a treat to get away for a week at Wakes Week for the lucky families who could afford the trip. The big rush started at Halifax station and were largely for the old favourite Blackpool and resorts on the Yorkshire coast.

This fantastic photograph is a snapshot of life in Halifax during the 'Roaring Twenties'. The picture was taken in Wards End, looking along towards Southgate and the Town Hall in the distance. The vintage car parked in the middle of the road behind the ornate gas street lamp, could well be a 'Model T' Ford produced after the First World War, in the early 1920s. The Registration No CP 4771 is the prefix for Halifax and Huddersfield, first introduced in 1903. On the right was the oldest theatre in Halifax built in 1790 and destroyed by a fire in 1904 after which it was rebuilt. The new Theatre Royal was opened by Alderman Enoch Robinson, the Mayor of Halifax on 4 August, 1905. Consisting of a superb façade in ashlar stone in the Edwardian style dates from this period, and was designed by Richard Horsfall & Son of Halifax. The theatre was converted for cinema and café use in 1933; then in the 1960s a bingo hall, before being converted into a nightclub. Women in the twenties did not leave the house without some form of head covering and in this photograph the headgear of choice seems to be the snug fitting cloche hat.

On the Move

A shot along Commercial Street in the 1930s presents a view which, architecturally, has altered little since that time. The fine domed building in the background, at present the NatWest Bank but at that time the National Provincial Bank, still catches the eye. To the left is the Classical style Lloyds Bank building, designed by Horsfall and Williams of Halifax, proud at its opening in 1898. To the right, from King Edward Street, emerges 'the old', in the shape of the horse and cart. At the far end of Commercial Street is 'the shape of things to come' - the motor car. The tram in the middle falls somewhere between the old and the new, for although it was one of the 21 'de-luxe' trams introduced between 1929 and 1931, its day was over almost before it had begun. All trams, 'de-luxe' or otherwise, were off the streets of Halifax by 1940.

This boneshaker of a motor car must have been one of the earliest ever seen in Calderdale. Amazingly, the cows in the field have taken it all in their stride. You would have thought the shock of seeing such a novel form of transport would have been enough to curdle the milk. The young man at the controls looks a little nervous as he clutches the horn, ready to warn unwary cyclists and pedestrians of his imminent arrival. Do you think that one of the smartly dressed women is his young lady and the other her chaperone, or is he merely the chauffeur? This very early car had a tiller instead of a steering wheel and was notoriously difficult to control. The steering wheel was not introduced until nearly 1900, though by the end of the Edwardian era all new cars had dispensed with tillers. Speed limits in towns were very restrictive. On 28 January, 1896, Walter Arnold, of East Peckham, Kent became the first person in Great Britain to be successfully charged with speeding. Travelling at approximately 8 mph, he had exceeded the 2 mph speed limit for towns and was fined a shilling (5p) plus costs.

The motorbike and sidecar is a fairly rare sight on our roads today. But, at one time they were quite popular. Quite how the woman passenger viewed her journey was not recorded, but she probably thought of it as being quite a thrilling experience. Hopefully, she did not come to grief as her headwear was more of a fashion statement than any sort of protection. Her friend on the pillion of the other bike was similarly adorned, but had the added problem of preserving her modesty when the wind whipped around those dainty ankles. This rider from Halifax has his sidecar fitted on the near-side (left side) of the motorcycle, however, up until 1981 there was no legal requirement for which side the sidecar should be fitted and some passengers may have endured a quite hair-raising experience in a right-sided sidecart with on-coming traffic whizzing past just an arms length away. Since 1981, under the UK law regarding the fitting of sidecars, any rider wishing to do so must have the sidecar fitted on the left side of the bike.

The formidable incline of Bolton Brow awaits tram No64 as a passenger mounts the platform. This is a remarkable photograph in a number of ways. Considering its date, 1905, it has very good definition so that the details of an Edwardian street scene stand out clearly - the gas lamps, the fashionable hats and long dresses. What is perhaps more remarkable is that the camera catches the very tramcar which was involved in a disaster, two years later, tackling this very ascent. The tram was climbing out of Sowerby Bridge with a full complement of around 60 passengers at 5.35 am. As the tramcar reached the top of Pye Nest, the electric current failed and it began to roll backwards at ever increasing speed.

The final extension to the Halifax tramway system was a very modest one - just a few hundred yards in 1925, to a terminus near the Standard of Freedom at Skircoat Green. Anyone who knows their Halifax will recognise the locality instantly. A mother and her children had just alighted from the tram ready to make the return journey to Pellon. Skircoat was an independent township before being absorbed by the Borough of Halifax in 1892. The name was originally Schircotes and means building on the rocks. It became an exclusive residential suburb for the 'upwardly mobile' of Halifax in the nineteenth century, and houses that can only be described as mansions were built. Louis John Crossley, for example, of the Dean Clough carpet dynasty, had a fully equipped laboratory and workshop in his Moorside home, and a tramway system in the grounds. Ironically, however, there was no escape, even at Skircoat, from the factory smoke that was creating the wealth to build the mansions. Henry Savile surrendered his manorial rights at Skircoat Moor (land valued at £40,000) to the Corporation for a nominal £100, one condition being that it tried t

The motor bus undertaking was beset by problems during the early years of operation. Not the least of these were the frequent interruptions to service, caused by accidents and breakdowns due to mechanical failure. On this particular occasion the No 2 bus travelling past Stansfield Bridge, Todmorden, on its way to the Town Hall, veered out of control and ran into the wall of Roomfield Chapel, after the steering collapsed. The incident took place on 18 March, 1907, some three months after the service began. Driver William Nothard was commended for remaining at his post, although his comment at the time may have us believe a slightly different story when he said "I couldn't get out of the damn thing!" Identifiable amongst the onlookers, who are seemingly more interested in the camera than the actual crash, are the local butcher Sam Newell and road sweeper Albert Heliwell.

'Oops' is perhaps the appropriate word to accompany this picture! We can tell from the black & white bollard in the distance that the accident happened during wartime. The car, possibly a Hillman Minx, could be a military vehicle, but it is unclear what and why the object is strapped to the roof. Whatever the reason, it has hit the shop front with considerable force. An alternative solution could be that this was some sort of unsuccessful 'smash & grab' raid on Lister Horsfall Jewellers. If that was the case, they would have to make their escape on foot as this car is going knowhere fast. The photograph was taken on Southgate looking along Cornmarket towards the Town Hall, which can be seen in the background of the shot. Lister Horsfall's were established in Halifax in 1902 and remain in this same spot, at the bottom of Cheapside, to this day.

Many readers will recall the view of King Cross shown here as it was in the late 1960s. This is the junction with Rochdale and Burnley Road before it was widened and flattened and filled with traffic lights and traffic lanes. Along the parade of shops, left hand side of the photograph, was Mrs Priestleys Toy Shop. Further along was Wendy's Fish and Chip shop. The Feathers, seen centre back of the photograph, still stands and Haugh Shaw Road leads off to the right. The 'Old King' pub is visible on the right of this picture. The well known Danny Gethins Pie Shop was across the road from the Old King. How many readers can remember visiting Danny's with a basket containing a pudding basin and a cloth. It was necessary to take your own container and a large pudding basin in a shopping basket provided stable carriage for the pie and peas you had to carry home. The cloth protected your supper and helped to keep it warm!

Here we have a busy traffic scene looking up King Cross Street from Bull Green. The once famous Courier clock tells us it is around 2.40pm and normally the traffic would be flowing freely….but not on this day. The vehicles on show appear to date this photograph to the mid-60s. The Harella van is waiting at the end of Carlton Place, next to the Co-op grocery store, poised to join the queuing traffic. Harella, later S. R. Gent, had a clothing manufacturers business at Croftmyl, West Parade, until the factory closed in 1979. The Courier building is well known to most of us, built around 1921 following the merger of the Halifax Courier and the Halifax Guardian. The offices were extended by acquisition of neighbouring properties on Regent Street. In 1977, the Courier occupied the whole of Regent Street when the new extension and the printing hall were built. Sadly, that has all changed now and the Courier along with the clock has long gone. The building has now been converted into flats.

Around 200 rail enthusiasts arrived at the old St Paul's station, at the junction of Queen's Road and Parkinson Lane, on 6 September, 1953. Here they are lovingly clustered around tank engine no 69430, and no doubt a mile or two of camera film was used up that day. The station itself had been closed to passenger traffic in 1917, remaining open as a goods depot until June, 1960. Even after 1917, however, joint Mackintosh and Crossley works outings to the seaside set off from St Paul's, and sometimes a circus train arrived there. St Paul's was once the terminus station of the Halifax High Level Railway which joined the Halifax to Queensbury line (opened in 1879) at Holmfield. The construction of the High Level line between 1888 and 1890 was an impressive piece of engineering on the part of the Great Northern Railway Company. Deep cuttings and a tunnel were required, and a ten-arch viaduct carried the line across the Hebble Valley to Wheatley. The last goods train ran to St Paul's in 1960, and the station was demolished in 1963.

Beacon Hill, to the right, frowns down on what still was very much an industrialised Halifax in 1963. So much so that 'Wakes Weeks', the summer holiday fortnight, could be regarded as a time when the town might be 'dead'. This period traditionally fell in early July; the mills closed down; people took their holidays. The steam train can be seen here moving out of the station, hauled by Stanier Class no 42964, was a holiday special to Llandudno, packed with Halifax folk hoping to find some sunshine and fun at the seaside. And what a grimy looking Halifax these holidaymakers were leaving behind, to which the smoke from the engine was liberally contributing. Clean Air Acts had begun in 1956, but the great clean-ups of stonework lay ahead. What surprises people were to find as a result of the sandblasting. For example, the blackened station building to the left, first opened in 1855 but expanded in 1885, has been transformed by cleaning and renovation into the wonderfully stylish structure that we see today. Disused as a station since 1971, much credit goes to Eureka Children's Museum for recognising the building's importance and including it in its plans.

Left: A very early photograph of a tram No107 making its way down Stock Lane from Highroad Well to Warley. At the time the picture was taken, additional track is being laid in the area of Warley Springs. This was near to the site of the Old Warley Springs Brewery originally known as the Victoria Brewery. It was acquired by James Alderson & Company in 1908. After World War I, the company got into financial difficulties and sold the business to Thomas Ramsden & Son Limited (1919). Patrick Bronte, father of Emily, Charlotte and Anne Bronte, lived for a time in Warley at a house called 'The Grange'. Wilfred Pickles and his wife Mabel were also residents of Warley for many years, and Wilfred could occasionally be seen enjoying a pint of Webster's beer in the village pub, The Maypole.

Below: This photograph from the late 1960s gives a clear view of the building of the tunnel at Ainley Top, over which the M62 would scythe its way between Hull and Liverpool. The drivers in this queue of cars are waiting patiently at the temporary traffic lights. This would be a situation they would have to deal with for a number of years to come, when the work first began on the mighty M62, the "Highway in the Sky" at Scammonden in 1966. The motorway was at least 10 years in the planning stages before work began on the highest motorway in the land. A director of contractors, Sir Alfred McAlpine & Son is quoted as saying, "The toughest motorway project there has been so far in Britain. The sort of challenge that civil engineers dream about…" The dream was eventually realised in October 1971, when the Queen officially opened the motorway.

Left: Warley is as delightful a village as it was in the interwar years when children hopped aboard the single decker bus that bounced along the cobbles as it took them to school. Its history goes back so far that it was included in the Domesday Book, where it was referred to as 'Werlafeslei'. Warley Town, as this particular area is known, was originally one of 23 townships in the old Halifax parish. It was also one of the largest, stretching down to Luddenden and over to Sowerby Bridge. It was made up of tiny hamlets and little farming communities. The Congregational Chapel was built in 1846, reflecting the Nonconformist traditions that were strong in the surrounding area. This provided a focus for the growth of the current village. The cottages built in front of the chapel were for the use of agricultural workers as the industrial revolution largely passed the village by, being centred down the valley where the water sources lay. The present Maypole Inn is a reminder of the great maypole, the last one ever seen in Calderdale, that was erected in front of the chapel in 1863. It replaced an earlier one that had been erected around 1814 to celebrate the defeat of Napoleon. Unfortunately, the one in the photograph only lasted about 25 years and was removed as it had deteriorated rather badly.

The tramline was something akin to that of a horizontal switchback ride as it snaked its way through George's Square in 1930. There is a trio of little lads standing dangerously on the tracks, involved in some deep conversation, so let us hope that they nipped out of the way before the next tram came along. In truth, the boys were fairly safe as the clanking of the trams was warning enough for even the hardest of hearing. The boys were probably from middle class families, if their clothes are anything to go by. The knickerbockers, Eton style collars and smart jackets suggest that their parents were not short of the readies. This was an era when people were still very class conscious. The working classes even had an inverted sense of snobbery, not wanting to be seen to adopt middle class values. Unfortunately, these working classes became the unemployed classes as the decade unfolded and the depression years kicked in with a vengeance.